Motivational Poems

Keep yourself motivated
Inspiring and positive thinking

Edited by

ROCIU DANIEL-EDUARD

Cover and book design by AGORA BOOKS

Ultimate Inspirational Collection
volume 2
Motivational Poems
*Keep yourself motivated
Inspiring and positive thinking*

Printed in the United States of America
First Printing: May 2014

ISBN: 1499658435
ISBN-13: 978-1499658439

DEDICATION

This book is dedicated to my wife, Elise

CONTENTS

The road not taken 13

It couldn't be done....................................15

A smile 17

If you think you are beaten....................19

Men whom men condemn as ill 20

Just one...21

If i had my child to raise over again 23

Don't quit..24

Promise yourself.....................................25

Follow your dream 26

My comfort zone 27

Start where you stand 29

Playing the game 31

All for the best 33

Why not you? 35

It's the journey that's important 38

You travel through life...40

Keep them close..43

Count that day lost...45

Life 47

The world is against me 49

My creed 51

Things work out..53

Influence 55

Before you 56

Do more 57

We must 58

May you have 61

Profit from failure 62

Handwriting on the wall 64

Success 66

The most beautiful flower.......................................68

Climb 'til your dream comes true 71

The guy in the glass 73

The challenge 75

My wage 76

Watch...77

Equipment 78

Don't dwell 80

Our deepest fear...81

The invitation 83

Hidden mystery 86

Look well to this day 88

Compassion 90

That i a better person may be 93

It takes courage 94

May you have enough 96

Self-control...98

Seeking for happiness 100

The things that count 102

The superwoman 104

You are my butterfly....................................107

Courage 109

Invictus 111

Solitude 113

The paradoxical commandments 115

Phenomenal woman 117

The invitation...120

Hope is the thing with feathers.........................123

In spite of war 124

Homage to my hips.......................................126

Mother to son 127

A father to his son 128

A cradle song...130

Index 131

Don't Quit

When things go wrong as they sometimes will,
When the road you're trudging seems all uphill,
When funds are low and the debts are high,
And you want to smile, but you have to sigh.
When care is pressing you down a bit.
Rest, if you must, but don't you quit.
Life is queer with its twists and turns
As every one of us sometimes learns.
And many a failure turns about
When he might have won had he stuck it out:
Don't give up though the pace seems slow -
You may succeed with another blow.
Success is failure turned inside out -
The silver tint of the clouds of doubt.
And you never can tell how close you are.
It may be near when it seems so far:
So stick to the fight when you're hardest hit
It's when things seem worst that you must not quit.

If

Rudyard Kipling

If you can keep your head when all about you

Are losing theirs and blaming it on you.

If you can trust yourself when all men doubt you,

But make allowance for their doubting too;

If you can wait and not be tired by waiting,

Or being lied about, don't deal in lies,

Or being hated, don't give way to hating,

And yet don't look too good, nor talk too wise:

If you can dream - and not make dreams your master;

If you can think - and not make thoughts your aim;

If you can meet with Triumph and Disaster

And treat these two impostors just the same;

If you can bear to hear the truth you've spoken

Twisted by knaves to make a trap for fools,

Or watch the things you gave your life to, broken,

And stoop and build 'em up with worn-out tools:

If you can make one heap of all your winnings

And risk it on one turn of pitch-and-toss,

And lose, and start again at your beginnings

And never breathe a word about your loss;

If you can force your heart and nerve and sinew

To serve your turn long after they are gone,

And so hold on when there is nothing in you

Except the Will which says to them: 'Hold on!'

If you can talk with crowds and keep your virtue,

Or walk with Kings - nor lose the common touch,

If neither foes nor loving friends can hurt you,

If all men count with you, but none too much;

If you can fill the unforgiving minute

With sixty seconds' worth of distance run,

Yours is the Earth and everything that's in it,

And - which is more - you'll be a Man, my son!

The Road Not Taken

Robert Frost

Two roads diverged in a yellow wood,

And sorry I could not travel both

And be one traveler, long I stood

And looked down one as far as I could

To where it bent in the undergrowth.

Then took the other, as just as fair,

And having perhaps the better claim,

Because it was grassy and wanted wear;

Though as for that the passing there

Had worn them really about the same.

And both that morning equally lay

In leaves no step had trodden black.

Oh, I kept the first for another day!

Yet knowing how way leads on to way,

I doubted if I should ever come back.

I shall be telling this with a sigh

Somewhere ages and ages hence:

Two roads diverged in a wood, and I--

I took the one less travelled by,

And that has made all the difference.

It Couldn't be Done

Edgar

Somebody said that it couldn't be done,

But, he with a chuckle replied

That "maybe it couldn't" but he would be one

Who wouldn't say so till he'd tried.

So he buckled right in with the trace of a grin

On his face. If he worried he hid it.

He started to sing as he tackled the thing

That couldn't be done, as he did it.

Somebody scoffed: "Oh, you'll never do that;

At least no one we know has done it";

But he took off his coat and he took off his hat,

And the first thing we knew he'd begun it.

With a lift of his chin and a bit of a grin,

Without any doubting or quiddit,

He started to sing as he tackled the thing

That couldn't be done, and he did it.

There are thousands to tell you it cannot be done,

There are thousands to prophesy failure;

There are thousands to point out to you, one by one,

The dangers that wait to assail you.

But just buckle right in with a bit of a grin,

Just take off your coat and go to it;

Just start to sing as you tackle the thing

That cannot be done, and you'll do it

It takes 42 [53] muscles to smile.

It happens in a flash and the memory of it sometimes lasts forever.

If you smile ☺ at someone it may or may not make there day 10x better.

Smiling is a sign of happiness

Smiles are contagious

Smiles relieve stress

A Smile

Author Unknown

creates

A smile costs nothing, but gives much–

It takes but a moment, but the memory of it usually lasts forever.

None are so rich that can get along without it–

And none are so poor but that can be made rich by it.

Smiling helps you get promoted

It enriches those who receive, without making poor those who give–

It creates sunshine in the home,

Fosters good will in business,

Happiness is a state of mind.

And is the best antidote for trouble–

And yet it cannot be begged, borrowed, or stolen, for it is of no value

Unless it is given away.

Smile often. ☺

Some people are too busy to give you a smile-

Give them one of yours-

For the good Lord knows that no one needs a smile so badly

As he or she who has no more smiles left to give.

Keep a smile
On!

If You Think You are Beaten

Walter D. Wintle

If you think you are beaten, you are.

If you think you dare not, you don't.

If you'd like to win but think you can't,

It's almost certain you won't.

Life's battles don't always go

To the stronger or faster man,

But sooner or later, the man who wins

Is the man who thinks he can.

Men Whom Men Condemn as Ill

Joaquin Miller

In men whom men condemn as ill

I find so much of goodness still,

In men whom men pronounce divine

I find so much of sin and blot,

I do not dare to draw a line

Between the two, where God has not.

Just One

Author Unknown

One song can spark a moment,

One flower can wake the dream

One tree can start a forest,

One bird can herald spring.

One smile begins a friendship,

One handclasp lifts a soul.

One star can guide a ship at sea,

One word can frame the goal

One vote can change a nation,

One sunbeam lights a room

One candle wipes out darkness,

One laugh will conquer gloom.

One step must start each journey.

One word must start each prayer.

One hope will raise our spirits,

One touch can show you care.

One voice can speak with wisdom,

One heart can know what's true,

One life can make a difference,

You see, it's up to you!

If I Had my Child To Raise Over Again

by Diane Loomans

If I had my child to raise all over again,

I'd build self-esteem first, and the house later.

I'd finger paint more, and point the finger less.

I would do less correcting and more connecting.

I'd take my eyes off my watch, and watch with my eyes.

I would care to know less and know to care more.

I'd take more hikes and fly more kites.

I'd stop playing serious, and seriously play.

I would run through more fields and gaze at more stars,

I'd do more hugging and less tugging.

I'd see the oak tree in the acorn more often,

I would be firm less often, and affirm much more.

I'd model less about the love of power,

And more about the power of love

Don't Quit

Author Unknown

When things go wrong as they sometimes will;

When the road you're trudging seems all uphill;

When the funds are low, and the debts are high;

And you want to smile, but you have to sigh;

When care is pressing you down a bit

Rest if you must, but don't you quit.

Success is failure turned inside out;

The silver tint of the clouds of doubt;

And you can never tell how close you are;

It may be near when it seems afar.

So, stick to the fight when you're hardest hit

It's when things go wrong that you mustn't quit.

Promise Yourself

Promise yourself to be so strong that nothing can disturb your peace of mind.

To talk health, happiness, and prosperity to every person you meet.

To make all your friends feel like there is something in them.

To look at the sunny side of everything and make your optimism come true.

To think only of the best, to work only for the best, and expect only the best.

To be just as enthusiastic about the success of others as you are about your own.

To forget the mistakes of the past and press on the greater achievements of the future.

To wear a cheerful countenance at all times and give every living person you meet a smile.

To give so much time to the improvement of yourself that you have no time to criticize others.

To be too large for worry, too noble for anger, and too strong for fear, and to happy to permit the presence of trouble.

Follow Your Dream

by Amanda Bradley

Follow your dream.

Take one step at a time and don't settle for less,

Just continue to climb.

Follow your dream.

If you stumble, don't stop and lose sight of your goal

Press to the top.

For only on top can we see the whole view,

Can we see what we've done and what we can do;

Can we then have the vision to seek something new,

Press on.

Follow your dream.

My Comfort Zone

Author Unknown

I used to have a comfort zone

where I knew I wouldn't fail.

The same four walls and busywork

were really more like jail.

I longed so much to do the things I'd never done before,

But stayed inside my comfort zone and paced the same old floor.

I said it didn't matter that I wasn't doing much.

I said I didn't care for things like commission checks and such.

I claimed to be so busy with the things inside the zone,

But deep inside I longed for something special of my own.

I couldn't let my life go by just watching others win.

I held my breath; I stepped outside and let the change begin.

I took a step and with new strength I'd never felt before,

I kissed my comfort zone goodbye and closed and locked the door.

If you're in a comfort zone,

afraid to venture out,

Remember that all winners were at one time filled with doubt.

A step or two and words of praise can make your dreams come true.

Reach for your future with a smile; success is there for you!

Start Where You Stand

Berton Braley

Start where you stand and never mind the past,

The past won't help you in beginning new,

If you have left it all behind at last

Why, that's enough, you're done with it, you're through;

This is another chapter in the book,

This is another race that you have planned,

Don't give the vanished days a backward look,

Start where you stand.

The world won't care about your old defeats

If you can start anew and win success;

The future is your time, and time is fleet

And there is much of work and strain and stress;

Forget the buried woes and dead despairs,

Here is a brand-new trial right at hand,

The future is for him who does and dares,

Start where you stand.

Playing The Game

Author Unknown

Life is a game with a glorious prize,

If we can only play it right.

It is give and take, build and break,

And often it ends in a fight;

But he surely wins who honestly tries

(Regardless of wealth or fame),

He can never despair who plays it fair

How are you playing the game?

Do you wilt and whine, if you fail to win

In the manner you think your due?

Do you sneer at the man in case that he can

And does, do better than you?

Do you take your rebuffs with a knowing grin?

Do you laugh tho' you pull up lame?

Does your faith hold true when the whole world's blue?

How are you playing the game?

Get into the thick of it - wade in, boys!

Whatever your cherished goal;

Brace up your will till your pulses thrill,

And you dare - to your very soul!

Do something more than make a noise;

Let your purpose leap into flame

As you plunge with a cry, "I shall do or die,"

Then you will be playing the game.

All for the Best

By Edgar A.

Things mostly happen for the best.

However hard it seems to-day,

When some fond plan has gone astray

Or, what you've wished for most is lost

An' you sit countin' up the cost

With eyes half-blind by tears o'grief

While doubt is chokin' out belief,

You'll find when all is understood

That what seemed bad was really good.

Life can't be counted in a day.

The present rain that will not stop

Next autumn means a bumper crop.

We wonder why some things must be-

Care's purpose we can seldom see-

An' yet long afterwards we turn

To view the past, an' then we learn

That what once filled our minds with doubt

Was good for us as it worked out.

I've never know an hour of care

But that I've later come to see

That it has brought some joy to me.

Even the sorrows I have borne,

Leavin' me lonely an' forlorn

An' hurt an' bruised an' sick at heart,

An' though I could not understand

Why I should bow to Death's command,

That it was really better so.

Things mostly happen for the best.

So narrow is our vision here

That we are blinded by a tear

An' stunned by every hurt an' blow

Which comes to-day to strike us low.

An' yet some day we turn an' find

That what seemed cruel once was kind.

Most things, I hold, are wisely planned

If we could only understand.

Why Not You?

By Steve Maraboli

Today, many will awaken with a fresh sense of inspiration. Why not you?

Today, many will open their eyes to the beauty that surrounds them. Why not you?

Today, many will choose to leave the ghost of yesterday behind and seize the immeasurable power of today. Why not you?

Today, many will break through the barriers of the past by looking at the blessings of the present. Why not you?

Today, for many the burden of self doubt and insecurity will be lifted by the security and confidence of empowerment. Why not you?

Today, many will rise above their believed limitations and make contact with their powerful innate strength. Why not you?

Today, many will choose to live in such a manner that they will be a positive role model for their children. Why not you?

Today, many will choose to free themselves from the personal imprisonment of their bad habits. Why not you?

Today, many will choose to live free of conditions and rules governing their own happiness. Why not you?

Today, many will find abundance in simplicity. Why not you?

Today, many will be confronted by difficult moral choices and they will choose to do what is right instead of what is beneficial. Why not you?

Today, many will decide to no longer sit back with a victim mentality, but to take charge of their lives and make positive changes. Why not you?

Today, many will take the action necessary to make a difference. Why not you?

Today, many will make the commitment to be a better mother, father, son, daughter, student, teacher, worker, boss, brother, sister, & so much more. Why not you?

Today is a new day!

Many will seize this day.

Many will live it to the fullest.

Why not you?

It's The Journey That's Important

By John McLeod

Life, sometimes so wearying

Is worth its weight in gold

The experience of traveling

Lends a wisdom that is old

Beyond our 'living memory'

A softly spoken prayer:

"It's the journey that's important,

Not the getting there!"

Ins and outs and ups and downs

Life's road meanders aimlessly?

Or so it seems, but somehow

Leads us where we need to be,

And being simply human

We oft question and compare...

"Is the journey so important

Or the getting there?"

And thus it's always been

That question pondered down the ages

By simple men with simple ways

To wise and ancient sages...

How sweet then, quietly knowing

Reaching destination fair:

"It's the journey that's important, Not the getting there!"

You Travel Through Life

Unknown

As you travel through life there are always those times

When decisions just have to be made,

When the choices are hard, and solutions seem scarce,

And the rain seems to soak your parade.

There are some situations where all you can do

Is simply let go and move on,

Gather your courage and choose a direction

That carries you toward a new dawn.

So pack up your troubles and take a step forward

The process of change can be tough,

But think about all the excitement ahead

There might be adventures you never imagined

Just waiting around the next bend,

And wishes and dreams just about to come true

Perhaps you'll find friendships that spring from new things

As you challenge your status quo,

And learn there are so many options in life,

Perhaps you'll go places you never expected

And see things that you've never seen,

Or travel to fabulous, faraway worlds

And wonderful spots in between!

Perhaps you'll find warmth and affection and caring

And somebody special who's there

To help you stay cantered and listen with interest

To stories and feelings you share.

Perhaps you'll find comfort in knowing your friends

Are supportive of all that you do,

And believe that whatever decisions you make,

They'll be the right choices for you.

So keep putting one foot in front of the other,

And taking your life day by day...

There's a brighter tomorrow that's just down the road -

Don't look back! You're not going that way!

Keep Them Close

Unknown

One day a mother died.

And on that clear, cold morning,

in the warmth of her bedroom,

the daughter was struck with

the pain of learning that sometimes

there isn't any more.

No more hugs, no more lucky moments to celebrate together,

no more phone calls just to chat, no more "just one minute."

Sometimes, what we care about the most goes away,

never to return before we can say good-bye, say "I Love You."

So while we have it ... it's best we love it .

And care for it and fix it when it's broken

and take good care of it when it's sick.

This is true for marriage ... and friendships!

And children with bad report cards;

and dogs with bad hips;

and aging parents and grandparents.

We keep them because they are worth it,

because we cherish them!

Some things we keep -

like a best friend who moved away

or a classmate we grew up with.

There are just some things that

make us happy, no matter what.

Life is important, and so are the people we know.

And so, keep them close!

Count That Day Lost

By George Eliot

If you sit down at set of sun

And count the acts that you have done,

And, counting, find

One self-denying deed, one word

That eased the heart of him who heard,

One glance most kind

That fell like sunshine where it went-

Then you may count that day well spent.

But if, through all the livelong day,

You've cheered no heart, by yea or nay-

If, through it all

You've nothing done that you can trace

That brought the sunshine to one face-

No act most small

That helped some soul and nothing cost-

Then count that day as worse than lost.

Life

by Nan Terrell Reed

They told me that Life could be just what I made it

Life could be fashioned and worn like a gown;

I, the designer, mine the decision

Whether to wear it with bonnet or crown.

And so I selected the prettiest pattern

Life should be made of the rosiest hue

Something unique, and a bit out of fashion,

One that perhaps would be chosen by few.

But other folks came and they leaned o'er my shoulder;

Someone questioned the ultimate cost;

Somebody tangled the thread I was using;

One day I found that my scissors were lost.

And somebody claimed the material faded;

Somebody said I'd be tired ere 'twas worn;

Somebody's fingers, too pointed and spiteful,

Snatched at the cloth, and I saw it was torn.

The World Is Against Me

By Edgar A. Guest

"The world is against me," he said with a sigh.

"Somebody stops every scheme that I try.

The world has me down and it's keeping me there;

I don't get a chance. Oh, the world is unfair!

When a fellow is poor then he can't get a show;

The world is determined to keep him down low."

"What of Abe Lincoln?" I asked. "Would you say

That he was much richer than you are to-day?

He hadn't your chance of making his mark,

And his outlook was often exceedingly dark;

Yet he clung to his purpose with courage most grim

And he got to the top. Was the world against him?"

"What of Ben Franklin? I've oft heard it said

That many a time he went hungry to bed.

He started with nothing but courage to climb,

But patiently struggled and waited his time.

He dangled awhile from real poverty's limb,

Yet he got to the top. Was the world against him?

"I could name you a dozen, yes, hundreds, I guess,

Of poor boys who've patiently climbed to success;

All boys who were down and who struggled alone,

Who'd have thought themselves rich if your fortune they'd known;

Yet they rose in the world you're so quick to condemn,

And I'm asking you now, was the world against them?"

My Creed

By Edgar A.

To live as gently as I can;

To be, no matter where, a man;

To take what comes of good or ill

And cling to faith and honor still;

To do my best, and let that stand

The record of my brain and hand;

And then, should failure come to me,

Still work and hope for victory.

To have no secret place wherein

I stoop unseen to shame or sin;

To be the same when I'm alone

As when my every deed is known

To live undaunted, unafraid

Of any step that I have made;

To be without pretense or sham

Exactly what men think I am.

To leave some simple mark behind

To keep my having lived in mind,

If enmity to aught I show,

To be an honest, generous foe,

To play my little part, nor whine

That greater honors are not mine.

This, I believe, is all I need

For my philosophy and creed.

Things Work Out

By Edgar A.

Because it rains when we wish it wouldn't,

Because men do what they often shouldn't,

Because crops fail, and plans go wrong

Some of us grumble all day long.

But somehow, in spite of the care and doubt,

It seems at last that things work out.

Because we lose where we hoped to gain,

Because we suffer a little pain,

Because we must work when we'd like to play

Some of us whimper along life's way.

But somehow, as day always follows the night,

Most of our troubles work out all right.

Because we cannot forever smile,

Because we must trudge in the dust awhile,

Because we think that the way is long

Some of us whimper that life's all wrong.

But somehow we live and our sky grows bright,

And everything seems to work out all right.

So bend to your trouble and meet your care,

For the clouds must break, and the sky grow fair.

Let the rain come down, as it must and will,

But keep on working and hoping still.

For in spite of the grumblers who stand about,

Somehow, it seems, all things work out.

Influence

By Joseph Norris

Drop a pebble in the water,

And its ripples reach out far;

And the sunbeams dancing on them

May reflect them to a star.

Give a smile to someone passing,

Thereby making his morning glad;

It may greet you in the evening

When your own heart may be sad.

Do a deed of simple kindness;

Though its end you may not see,

It may reach, like widening ripples,

Down a long eternity.

Before You

By William Arthur Ward

Before you speak, listen.

Before you write, think.

Before you spend, earn.

Before you invest, investigate.

Before you criticize, wait.

Before you pray, forgive.

Before you quit, try.

Before you retire, save.

Before you die, give.

Do More

By William Arthur Ward

Do more than belong: participate.

Do more than care: help.

Do more than believe: practice.

Do more than be fair: be kind.

Do more than forgive: forget.

Do more than dream: work.

We Must

By William Arthur Ward

We must be silent before we can listen.

We must listen before we can learn.

We must learn before we can prepare.

We must prepare before we can serve.

We must serve before we can lead.

Be The Best of Whatever You Are

By Douglas Malloch

If you can't be a pine on the top of the hill,

Be a scrub in the valley-but be

The best little scrub by the side of the rill;

Be a bush if you can't be a tree.

If you can't be a bush be a bit of the grass,

And some highway happier make;

If you can't be a muskie then just be a bass

But the liveliest bass in the lake!

We can't all be captains, we've got to be crew,

There's something for all of us here,

There's big work to do, and there's lesser to do,

And the task you must do is the near.

If you can't be a highway then just be a trail,

If you can't be the sun be a star;

It isn't by size that you win or you fail

Be the best of whatever you are!

May You Have

Unknown

May you have......

Enough happiness to keep you sweet,

Enough trials to keep you strong,

Enough sorrow to keep you human,

Enough hope to keep you happy;

Enough failure to keep you humble,

Enough success to keep you eager,

Enough friends to give you comfort,

Enough wealth to meet your needs;

Enough enthusiasm to look forward,

Enough faith to banish depression,

Enough determination to make each day better than yesterday.

Profit From Failure

Unknown

The test of a man is the fight he makes,

The grit that he daily shows;

The way he stands on his feet and takes

Fate's numerous bumps and blows.

A coward can smile when there's naught to fear,

When nothing his progress bars;

But it takes a man to stand up and cheer

While some other fellow stars.

It isn't the victory, after all,

But the fight that a brother makes;

The man who, driven against the wall,

Still stands up erect and takes

The blows of fate with his head held high;

Bleeding, and bruised, and pale,

Is the man who'll win in the by and by,

For he isn't afraid to fail.

It's the bumps you get, and the jolts you get,

And the shocks that your courage stands,

The hours of sorrow and vain regret,

The prize that escapes your hands,

That test your mettle and prove your worth;

It isn't the blows you deal,

But the blows you take on the good old earth,

That show if your stuff is real.

Handwriting On The Wall

Unknown

A weary mother returned from the store,

Lugging groceries through the kitchen door.

Awaiting her arrival was her 8 year old son,

Anxious to relate what his younger brother had done.

While I was out playing and Dad was on a call,

T.J. took his crayons and wrote on the wall

It's on the new paper you just hung in the den.

I told him you'd be mad at having to do it again.

She let out a moan and furrowed her brow,

Where is your little brother right now?

She emptied her arms and with a purposeful stride,

She marched to his closet where he had gone to hide.

She called his full name as she entered his room.

He trembled with fear--he knew that meant doom

For the next ten minutes, she ranted and raved

About the expensive wallpaper and how she had saved.

Lamenting all the work it would take to repair,

She condemned his actions and total lack of care.

The more she scolded, the madder she got,

Then stomped from his room, totally distraught.

She headed for the den to confirm her fears.

When she saw the wall, her eyes flooded with tears.

The message she read pierced her soul with a dart.

It said, I love Mommy, surrounded by a heart.

Well, the wallpaper remained, just as she found it,

With an empty picture frame hung to surround it.

A reminder to her, and indeed to all,

Take time to read the handwriting on the wall.

Success

Unknown

Success is speaking words of praise,

In cheering other people's ways.

In doing just the best you can,

With every task and every plan.

It's silence when your speech would hurt,

Politeness when your neighbor's curt.

It's deafness when the scandal flows,

And sympathy with others' woes.

It's loyalty when duty calls,

It's courage when disaster falls.

It's patience when the hours are long,

It's found in laughter and in song.

It's in the silent time of prayer,

In happiness and in despair.

In all of life and nothing less,

We find the thing we call success.

The Most Beautiful Flower

Unknown

The park bench was deserted as I sat down to read

Beneath the long, straggly branches of an old willow tree.

Disillusioned by life with good reason to frown,

For the world was intent on dragging me down.

And if that weren't enough to ruin my day,

A young boy out of breath approached me, all tired from play.

He stood right before me with his head tilted down

And said with great excitement, "Look what I found!"

In his hand was a flower, and what a pitiful sight,

With its petals all worn - not enough rain, or too little light.

Wanting him to take his dead flower and go off to play,

I faked a small smile and then shifted away.

But instead of retreating he sat next to my side

And placed the flower to his nose and declared with overacted surprise,

"It sure smells pretty and it's beautiful, too.

That's why I picked it; here, it's for you."

The weed before me was dying or dead.

Not vibrant of colors: orange, yellow or red.

But I knew I must take it, or he might never leave.

So I reached for the flower, and replied, "Just what I need."

But instead of him placing the flower in my hand,

He held it mid-air without reason or plan.

It was then that I noticed for the very first time

That weed-toting boy could not see: he was blind.

I heard my voice quiver; tears shone in the sun

As I thanked him for picking the very best one.

"You're welcome," he smiled, and then ran off to play.

Unaware of the impact he'd had on my day.

I sat there and wondered how he managed to see

A self-pitying woman beneath an old willow tree.

How did he know of my self-indulged plight?

Perhaps from his heart, he'd been blessed with true sight.

Through the eyes of a blind child, at last I could see.

The problem was not with the world; the problem was me.

And for all of those times I myself had been blind,

I vowed to see the beauty in life,

And appreciate every second that's mine.

And then I held that wilted flower up to my nose

And breathed in the fragrance of a beautiful rose

And smiled as I watched that young boy,

Another weed in his hand,

About to change the life of an unsuspecting old man.

Climb 'Til Your Dream Comes True

Helen Steiner Rice

Often your tasks will be many,

And more than you think you can do.

Often the road will be rugged

And the hills insurmountable, too.

But always remember,

The hills ahead

Are never as steep as they seem,

And with Faith in your heart

Start upward

And climb 'til you reach your dream.

For nothing in life that is worthy

Is ever too hard to achieve

If you have the courage to try it,

And you have the faith to believe.

For faith is a force that is greater

Than knowledge or power or skill,

And many defeats turn to triumph

If you trust in God's wisdom and will.

For faith is a mover of mountains,

There's nothing that God cannot do,

So, start out today with faith in your heart,

And climb 'til your dream comes true!

The Guy in the Glass

by Dale Wimbrow

When you get what you want in your struggle for self

And the world makes you king for a day

Just go to the mirror and look at yourself

And see what that man has to say.

For it isn't your Father or Mother or wife

Whose judgment upon you must pass.

The fellow whose verdict counts most in your life

Is the one staring back from the glass.

Some people may call you a straight shooting chum

And call you a wonderful guy,

but the man in the glass says you're only a bum

If you can't look him straight in the eye.

He's the fellow to please, never mind all the rest

For he's with you clear to the end,

And you have passed your most dangerous test

If the man in the glass is your friend.

You may face the whole world down the pathway of life

And get pats on the back when you pass,

But your final reward will be heartache and strife

If you've cheated the man in the glass.

The Challenge

by Jim Rohn

Let others lead small lives,

But not you.

Let others argue over small things,

But not you.

Let others cry over small hurts,

But not you.

Let others leave their future

In someone else's hands,

But not you.

My Wage

by Jessie B. Rittenhouse

I bargained with life for a penny,

And life would pay no more,

However I begged at evening

When I counted my scanty store;

For life is a just employer,

He gives you what you ask,

But once you have set the wages,

Why, you must bear the task.

I worked for a menial's hire,

Only to learn dismayed,

That any wage I had asked of life,

Life would have paid.

Watch

By Frank Outlaw

Watch your thoughts, for they become words.

Watch your words, for they become actions.

Watch your actions, for they become habits.

Watch your habits, for they become character.

Watch your character, for it becomes your destiny.

Equipment

By Edgar A.

Figure it out for yourself, my lad,

You've all that the greatest of men have had,

Two arms, two hands, two legs, two eyes

And a brain to use if you would be wise.

With this equipment they all began,

So start for the top and say, "I can."

Look them over, the wise and great

They take their food from a common plate,

And similar knives and forks they use,

With similar laces they tie their shoes.

The world considers them brave and smart,

But you've all they had when they made their start.

You can triumph and come to skill,

You can be great if you only will.

You're well equipped for what fight you choose,

You have legs and arms and a brain to use,

And the man who has risen great deeds to do

Began his life with no more than you.

You are the handicap you must face,

You are the one who must choose your place,

You must say where you want to go,

How much you will study the truth to know.

God has equipped you for life, but He

Lets you decide what you want to be.

Courage must come from the soul within,

The man must furnish the will to win.

So figure it out for yourself, my lad.

You were born with all that the great have had,

With your equipment they all began,

Get hold of yourself and say: "I can."

Don't Dwell

Author Unknown

Don't dwell on what might have been or the chances you have missed.

Or the lonely nights that lie between the last time lovers kissed.

Don't grasp too hard the memory of the things that never came.

The door that did not open or the wind that killed the flame.

There is still time enough to live...And time enough to try again.

Be Happy.

Our Deepest Fear

By Marianne Williamson

Our deepest fear is not that we are inadequate.

Our deepest fear is that we are powerful beyond measure.

It is our light, not our darkness

That most frightens us.

We ask ourselves

Who am I to be brilliant, gorgeous, talented, fabulous?

Actually, who are you not to be?

You are a child of God.

Your playing small

Does not serve the world.

There's nothing enlightened about shrinking

So that other people won't feel insecure around you.

We are all meant to shine,

As children do.

We were born to make manifest

The glory of God that is within us.

It's not just in some of us;

It's in everyone.

And as we let our own light shine,

We unconsciously give other people permission to do the same.

As we're liberated from our own fear,

Our presence automatically liberates others.

The Invitation

By Oriah Mountain Dreamer

It doesn't interest me what you do for a living.

I want to know what you ache for,

And if you dare to dream of meeting

Your heart's longing.

It doesn't interest me how old you are.

I want to know if you will risk looking like a fool

For love, for your dream,

For the adventure of being alive.

It doesn't interest me what planets are squaring your moon.

I want to know if you have touched the center of your own sorrow,

If you have been opened by life's betrayals,

Or have become shriveled and closed from fear of further pain.

I want to know if you can sit with pain,

Mine or your own,

Without moving

To hide it or fade it or fix it.

I want to know if you can be with joy,

Mine or your own,

If you can dance with wildness

and let the ecstasy fill you to the tips of your fingers and toes

Without cautioning us to be careful, be realistic,

or to remember the limitations of being human.

It doesn't interest me if the story you are telling me is true.

I want to know if you can disappoint another to be true to yourself,

If you can bear the accusation of betrayal and not betray your own soul.

I want to know if you can be faithless and therefore be trustworthy.

I want to know if you can see beauty

Even when it is not pretty every day,

And if you can source your life

From its presence.

I want to know if you can live with failure,

Yours and mine,

And still stand on the edge of a lake and shout to the silver of the full moon,

"Yes!"

It doesn't interest me to know where you live or how much money you have.

I want to know if you can get up after the night of grief and despair,

Weary and bruised to the bone,

And do what needs to be done for the children.

It doesn't interest me who you are, how you came to be here.

I want to know if you will stand

In the center of the fire with me

And not shrink back.

It doesn't interest me where or what or with whom you have studied.

I want to know what sustains you

From the inside

When all else falls away.

I want to know if you can be alone

With yourself,

And if you truly like the company you keep

In the empty moments.

Hidden Mystery

By Fred Burks

In the deepest depths of you and me

In the deepest depths of we

Lies the most beautiful jewel

Shining forth eternally

Within that precious jewel

Within that priceless piece of we

Lies a time beyond all time

Lies a place beyond all space

Within that sacred source of radiance

Lies a love beyond all love

Waiting

Waiting

Waiting

Ever so patiently

Waiting for you, waiting for me

Waiting patiently for all to see

The beauty that is you inside of me

The beauty that is me inside of thee

In the deepest depths of you and me

In the deepest depths of we

Lies the love and wisdom

Of all Eternity

Look Well to This Day

Anonymous, 50 B.C.

Look well to this day,

For it and it alone is life.

In its brief course

Lie all the essence of your existence:

The Glory of Growth

The Satisfaction of Achievement

The Splendor of Beauty

For yesterday is but a dream,

And tomorrow is but a vision.

But today well lived makes every yesterday a dream of happiness,

And every tomorrow a vision of hope.

The Serenity Prayer

By Reinhold Neibuhr

God grant that I might have

The courage to change the things I can,

The serenity to accept the things I cannot,

And the wisdom to know the difference

Compassion

Angels must be confused by war.

Both sides praying for protection,

yet someone always gets hurt.

Someone dies.

Someone cries so deep

they lose their watery state.

Angels must be confused by war.

Who can they help?

Who can they clarify?

Whose mercy do they cast to the merciless?

No modest scream can be heard.

No stainless pain can be felt.

All is clear to angels

except in war.

When I awoke to this truth,

it was from a dream I had last night.

I saw two angels conversing in a field

of children's spirits rising like silver smoke.

The angels were fighting among themselves

about which side was right,

and which was wrong.

Who started the conflict?

Suddenly, the angels stilled themselves

like a stalled pendulum,

and they shed their compassion

to the rising smoke

of souls who bore the watermark of war.

They turned to me with those eyes

from God's library,

and all the pieces fallen

were raised in unison,

intertwined like the breath

of flames in a holy furnace.

Nothing in war comes to destruction,

but the illusion of separateness.

I heard this spoken so clearly I could only

write it down like a forged signature.

I remember the compassion,

mountainous, proportioned for the universe.

I think a tiny fleck still sticks to me,

like gossamer threads

from a spider's web.

And now, when I think of war,

I flick these threads to all the universe,

hoping they stick on others as they did me.

Knitting angels and animals

to the filamental grace of compassion.

The reticulum of our skyward home.

That I A Better Person May Be

Author Unknown

Light that lies deep inside of me

Come forth in all thy majesty

Show me thy gaze

Teach me thy ways

That I a better person may be

Darkness that lies deep inside of me

Come forth in all thy mystery

Show me thy gaze

Teach me thy ways

That I a better person may be

Love that lies deep inside of me

Come forth in all thy unity

Let me be thy gaze

Let me teach thy ways

That I a better person may be

It Takes Courage

by Author Unknown

It takes strength to be firm,

It takes courage to be gentle.

It takes strength to conquer,

It takes courage to surrender.

It takes strength to be certain,

It takes courage to have doubt.

It takes strength to fit in,

It takes courage to stand out.

It takes strength to feel a friend's pain,

It takes courage to feel your own pain.

It takes strength to endure abuse,

It takes courage to stop it.

It takes strength to stand alone,

It takes courage to lean on another.

It takes strength to love,

It takes courage to be loved.

It takes strength to survive,

It takes courage to live.

May You Have Enough

by Fion Lim

May you have a healthy body,

To move around freely and roam wherever you desire to go.

May you have good vision,

To enjoy all the beauty the universe has to offer you.

May you have good listening ears,

To hear all the mighty tales and incredible stories that make up life.

May you have a good sense of smell,

To inhale in all the rich aromas and fragrances floating in the air.

May you have a warm sense of touch,

To give out loving hugs and comforting pats.

May you speak with kindness from your heart,

To soothe someone's hurt and to uplift someone's mood.

May you have lots of laughter,

To brighten up someone's day and make a difference.

May you have lots of courage,

To go after your dreams and turn them into reality.

May you have lots of love,

To spread around and leaving this world a better place.

May you have enough to feel blessed,

And to share your gift of blessings with others too.

Self-Control

by Author Unknown

I've heard it said don't go to bed

while hanging on to sorrow,

you may not have the chance to laugh

with those you love tomorrow.

You may not mean the words you speak

when anger takes its toll,

you may regret your actions

once you've lost your self-control.

When you've lost your temper

and you've said some hurtful things,

think about the heartache

that your actions sometimes bring.

You'll never get those moments back,

such precious time to waste,

and all because of things you said

in anger and in haste.

So if you really love someone

and your pride has settled in,

you may not ever have the chance

to say to them again....

"I love you and I miss you,

and although we don't agree,

I'll try to see your point of view,

please do the same for me."

Seeking for Happiness

Ella Wheeler Wilcox

Seeking for happiness we must go slowly;

The road leads not down avenues of haste;

But often gently winds through by ways lowly,

Whose hidden pleasures are serene and chaste

Seeking for happiness we must take heed

Of simple joys that are not found in speed.

Eager for noon-time's large effulgent splendor,

Too oft we miss the beauty of the dawn,

Which tiptoes by us, evanescent, tender,

Its pure delights unrecognized till gone.

Seeking for happiness we needs must care

For all the little things that make life fair.

Dreaming of future pleasures and achievements

We must not let to-day starve at our door;

Nor wait till after losses and bereavements

Before we count the riches in our store.

Seeking for happiness we must prize this -

Not what will be, or was, but that which is.

In simple pathways hand in hand with duty

(With faith and love, too, ever at her side),

May happiness be met in all her beauty

The while we search for her both far and wide.

Seeking for happiness we find the way

Doing the things we ought to do each day.

The Things That Count

lla Wheeler Wilcox

Now, dear, it isn't the bold things,

Great deeds of valor and might,

That count the most in the summing up of life at the end of the day.

But it is the doing of old things,

Small acts that are just and right;

And doing them over and over again, no matter what others say;

In smiling at fate, when you want to cry, and in keeping at work when you want to play -

Dear, those are the things that count.

And, dear, it isn't the new ways

Where the wonder-seekers crowd

That lead us into the land of content, or help us to find our own.

But it is keeping to true ways,

Though the music is not so loud,

And there may be many a shadowed spot where we journey along alone;

In flinging a prayer at the face of fear, and in changing into a song
a groan -

Dear, these are the things that count.

My dear, it isn't the loud part

Of creeds that are pleasing to God,

Not the chant of a prayer, or the hum of a hymn, or a jubilant
shout or song.

But it is the beautiful proud part

Of walking with feet faith-shod;

And in loving, loving, loving through all, no matter how things go
wrong;

In trusting ever, though dark the day, and in keeping your hope
when the way seems long -

Dear, these are the things that count.

The Superwoman

Ella Wheeler Wilcox

What will the superwoman be, of whom we sing -

She who is coming over the dim border

Of Far To-morrow, after earth's disorder

Is tidied up by Time? What will she bring

To make life better on tempestuous earth?

How will her worth

Be greater than her forbears? What new power

Within her being will burst into flower?

She will bring beauty, not the transient dower

Of adolescence which departs with youth -

But beauty based on knowledge of the truth

Of its eternal message and the source

Of all its potent force.

Her outer being by the inner thought

Shall into lasting loveliness be wrought.

She will bring virtue; but it will not be

The pale, white blossom of cold chastity

Which hides a barren heart. She will be human -

Not saint or angel, but the superwoman -

Mother and mate and friend of superman.

She will bring strength to aid the larger Plan,

Wisdom and strength and sweetness all combined,

Drawn from the Cosmic Mind -

Wisdom to act, strength to attain,

And sweetness that finds growth in joy or pain.

She will bring that large virtue, self-control,

And cherish it as her supremest treasure.

Not at the call of sense or for man's pleasure

Will she invite from space an embryo soul,

To live on earth again in mortal fashion,

Unless love stirs her with divinest passion.

To motherhood she will bring common sense -

That most uncommon virtue. She will give

Love that is more than she-wolf violence

(Which slaughters others that its own may live).

Love that will help each little tendril mind

To grow and climb;

Love that will know the lordliest use of Time

In training human egos to be kind.

She will be formed to guide, but not to lead -

Leaders are ever lonely - and her sphere

Will be that of the comrade and the mate,

Loved, loving, and with insight fine and clear,

Which casts its searchlight on the course of fate,

And to the leaders says, 'Proceed' or 'Wait.'

And best of all, she will bring holy faith

To penetrate the shadowy world of death,

And show the road beyond it, bright and broad,

That leads straight up to God.

You Are My Butterfly

by Tanja Cilia

You Are......... My Butterfly

You brought color to my life....

You helped me to select the sweet from the bitter

And savor the moment.

You showed me how to take things lightly

You helped me soar above

My worries.

You helped me spread my wings

And notice the flowers.

You are my butterfly, and I love you.

You showed me it's true that if

You chase a butterfly, away he flies;

But if you sit still, he brushes your cheek

With his wings and changes the

Monochrome vistas of grey

Into a suffusion of color.

Never were poppies so crimson

Or daffodils so yellow

As now.

Green apples and honey

Mint and liquorice and ginger, and

Stamens of the honeysuckle

Were never so real.

You are my butterfly.

Diving into the cool water

Feeling the warmth of a puppy

Touching an empty cocoon

Listening to the rain

Seeing the sun set

Hearing the rustle of leaves

Were never so aesthetic and sensual

As they has become since I

Met you.

For you are

My Butterfly.

You are my inspiration, the love of

My Life.

My Butterfly.

Courage

by Fion Lim

Courage is not only gifted to the few brave ones,

It is something that lies within you,

Where you can draw upon its strength and power,

In times of crisis, fears and decisions.

Courage is not something mysterious or unattainable,

It is something that you can exercise in your daily life choices,

You can let it bring to you untraveled paths,

And make you more conscious and aware of your life.

Courage does not have to roar to be heard,

It does not mean being totally fearless and being invincible,

It could mean taking actions, taking risks, taking a stand,

Standing up for yourself, standing by your choices,

And sticking to your dreams when others jeered.

Courage could be the will to live in spite of the struggles,

In spite of your fears and phobias, in spite of what others said,

In spite of criticisms and disapproval, in spite of mistakes and failures,

In spite of everything that stands between you and your dreams.

Courage could mean trying over and over again when you failed,

Admitting that you are sorry when you are in the wrong,

Saying I love you when your love is angry,

Having a baby when the idea of being a parent scared you,

Listening to your heart when others called you a fool,

Following your dreams even when others discouraged you,

And staying true to yourself when others want you in another way.

Hold steadfast to your dreams, your heart and yourself,

And courage will not abandon you,

But follows you whenever you choose to go.

Invictus

By William Ernest Henley[1]

Out of the night that covers me,
Black as the Pit from pole to pole,
I thank whatever gods may be
For my unconquerable soul.

In the fell clutch of circumstance
I have not winced nor cried aloud.
Under the bludgeonings of chance
My head is bloody, but unbowed.

---

[1] *We are the master of our destiny. We are responsible for our own happiness. This famous inspirational poem charges us to accept responsibility for our lives no matter our circumstances. Invictus in Latin means unconquered. William Ernest Henley (1849–1903), an English Poet, had one of his legs amputated at the age of 17. The poem which he wrote while healing from the amputation is a testimony to his refusal to let his handicap disrupt his life. Indeed, he led a meaningful life as a poet and editor until he passed away at age 53.*

It matters not how strait the gate,
How charged with punishments the scroll,
I am the master of my fate:
I am the captain of my soul.

Solitude

By Ella Wheeler Wilcox[2]

Laugh, and the world laughs with you;
Weep, and you weep alone;
For the sad old earth must borrow its mirth,
But has trouble enough of its own.
Sing, and the hills will answer;
Sigh, it is lost on the air;
The echoes bound to a joyful sound,
But shrink from voicing care.

Rejoice, and men will seek you;

~~Grieve, and they turn and go;~~

[2] ". The poem was first published in a 1883 issue of The New York Sun and it is Ella Wheeler Wilcox's most famous poem. The idea for the poem came as she was travelling to Madison, Wisconsin to attend the Governor's inaugural ball. On her way to the celebration, there was a young woman dressed in black sitting across the aisle from her. The woman was crying. Miss Wheeler sat next to her and sought to comfort her for the rest of the journey. When they arrived, the poet was so unhappy that she could barely attend the festivities. As she looked at her own face in the mirror, she suddenly recalled the sorrowful widow. It was at that moment that she wrote the opening lines of "Solitude.

But alone you must drink life's gall.

Feast, and your halls are crowded;
Fast, and the world goes by.
Succeed and give, and it helps you live,
But no man can help you die.
There is room in the halls of pleasure
For a large and lordly train,
But one by one we must all file on
Through the narrow aisles of pain.

The Paradoxical Commandments

By Kent M. Keith[3]

People are illogical, unreasonable, and self-centered.
Love them anyway.

If you do good, people will accuse you of selfish ulterior motives.
Do good anyway.

If you are successful, you will win false friends and true enemies.
Succeed anyway.

The good you do today will be forgotten tomorrow.
Do good anyway.

Honesty and frankness make you vulnerable.

3 *This selection, entitled, "The Paradoxical Commandments", was written by Kent M. Keith in 1968 when he was a 19 year old Harvard Student. Since then, it has been quoted by millions and even mistakenly attributed to Mother Teresa who had a version hung as a poem on a wall in her Children's Home in Calcutta. The text contains 10 commandments. The theme and the paradox is to persevere in doing good for humanity and acting with integrity even if your efforts aren't appreciated.*

Think big anyway.

People favor underdogs but follow only top dogs.
Fight for a few underdogs anyway.

What you spend years building may be destroyed overnight.
Build anyway.

People really need help but may attack you if you do help them.
Help people anyway.

Give the world the best you have and you'll get kicked in the teeth.
Give the world the best you have anyway.

Phenomenal Woman

By Maya Angelou[4]

Pretty women wonder where my secret lies.
I'm not cute or built to suit a fashion model's size
But when I start to tell them,
They think I'm telling lies.
I say,
It's in the reach of my arms
The span of my hips,
The stride of my step,
The curl of my lips.
I'm a woman
Phenomenally.
Phenomenal woman,
That's me.

I walk into a room
Just as cool as you please,
And to a man,
The fellows stand or

4 *This poem shows how even though someone is not beautiful on the outside compared to society's standards, there is an inner beauty that makes a woman even more beautiful.*

A hive of honey bees.
I say,
It's the fire in my eyes,
And the flash of my teeth,
The swing in my waist,
And the joy in my feet.
I'm a woman
Phenomenally.
Phenomenal woman,
That's me.

Men themselves have wondered
What they see in me.
They try so much
But they can't touch
My inner mystery.
When I try to show them
They say they still can't see.
I say,
It's in the arch of my back,
The sun of my smile,
The ride of my breasts,
The grace of my style.
I'm a woman

Phenomenally.
Phenomenal woman,
That's me.

Now you understand
Just why my head's not bowed.
I don't shout or jump about
Or have to talk real loud.
When you see me passing
It ought to make you proud.
I say,
It's in the click of my heels,
The bend of my hair,
the palm of my hand,
The need of my care,

'Cause I'm a woman
Phenomenally.
Phenomenal woman,
That's me.

The Invitation

By Oriah Mountain Dreamer

It doesn't interest me
what you do for a living.
I want to know
what you ache for
and if you dare to dream
of meeting your heart's longing.

It doesn't interest me
how old you are.
I want to know
if you will risk
looking like a fool
for love
for your dream
for the adventure of being alive.

It doesnt interest me
what planets are
squaring your moon...
I want to know
if you have touched
the centre of your own sorrow
if have been opened
by life's betrayals
or have become shrivelled and closed
from fear of further pain.

I want to know
if you can sit with pain

mine or your own
without moving to hide it
or fade it
or fix it.

I want to know
if you can be with joy
mine or your own
if you can dance with wildness
and let the ecstasy fill you
to the tips of your fingers and toes
without cautioning us
to be careful
to be realistic
to remember the limitations
of being human.

It doesn't interest me
if the story you are telling me
is true.
I want to know if you can
disappoint another
to be true to yourself.
If you can bear
the accusation of betrayal
and not betray your own soul.
If you can be faithless
and therefore trustworthy.

I want to know if you can see Beauty
even when it is not pretty
every day.
And if you can source your own life
from its presence.

I want to know
if you can live with failure
yours and mine
and still stand at the edge of the lake
and shout to the silver of the full moon,

"Yes."

It doesn't interest me
to know where you live
or how much money you have.
I want to know if you can get up
after the night of grief and despair
weary and bruised to the bone
and do what needs to be done
to feed the children.

It doesn't interest me
who you know
or how you came to be here.
I want to know if you will stand
in the centre of the fire
with me
and not shrink back.

It doesn't interest me
where or what or with whom
you have studied.
I want to know
what sustains you
from the inside
when all else falls away.

I want to know
if you can be alone
with yourself
and if you truly like
the company you keep
in the empty moments.

Hope Is The Thing With Feathers

By Emily Dickinson[5]

"Hope" is the thing with feathers -
That perches in the soul -
And sings the tune without the words -
And never stops - at all -

And sweetest - in the Gale - is heard -
And sore must be the storm -
That could abash the little Bird
That kept so many warm -

I've heard it in the chillest land -
And on the strangest Sea -
Yet - never - in Extremity,
It asked a crumb - of me.

---

5 *In this Metaphor poem, the bird is a symbol for hope. Emily Dickinson, born in 1830 in Amherst, Massachusetts, is the author of almost 2000 poems. Only after she died in 1886 were her poems discovered.*

In Spite of War

By Angela Morgan

In spite of war, in spite of death,
In spite of all man's sufferings,
Something within me laughs and sings
And I must praise with all my breath.
In spite of war, in spite of hate
Lilacs are blooming at my gate,
Tulips are tripping down the path
In spite of war, in spite of wrath.
"Courage!" the morning-glory saith;
"Rejoice!" the daisy murmureth,
And just to live is so divine
When pansies lift their eyes to mine.

The clouds are romping with the sea,
And flashing waves call back to me
That naught is real but what is fair,
That everywhere and everywhere
A glory lived through despair.
Though guns may roar and cannon boom,
Roses are born and gardens bloom;
My spirit still may light its flame
At that same torch whence poppies came.
Where morning's altar whitely burns
Lilies may lift their silver urns
In spite of war, in spite of shame.

And in my ear a whispering breath,

"Wake from the nightmare! Look and see
That life is naught but ecstasy
In spite of war, in spite of death!"

Homage To My Hips

By Lucille Clifton

these hips are big hips
they need space to
move around in.
they don't fit into little
petty places. these hips
are free hips.
they don't like to be held back.
these hips have never been enslaved,
they go where they want to go
they do what they want to do.
these hips are mighty hips.
these hips are magic hips.
i have known them
to put a spell on a man and
spin him like a top!

Mother To Son

By Langston Hughes[6]

Well, son, I'll tell you:
Life for me ain't been no crystal stair.
It's had tacks in it,
And splinters,
And boards torn up,
And places with no carpet on the floor—
Bare.
But all the time
I'se been a-climbin' on,
And reachin' landin's,
And turnin' corners,
And sometimes goin' in the dark
Where there ain't been no light.
So, boy, don't you turn back.
Don't you set down on the steps.
'Cause you finds it's kinder hard.
Don't you fall now—
For I'se still goin', honey,
I'se still climbin',
And life for me ain't been no crystal stair.

---

[6] *In this poem, a mother uses the metaphor of life being like a staircase to give advice to her son. While there are difficult times, you must keep moving like you would while walking up a staircase*

A Father To His Son

By Carl Sandburg[7]

A father sees his son nearing manhood.
What shall he tell that son?
"Life is hard; be steel; be a rock."
And this might stand him for the storms
and serve him for humdrum monotony
and guide him among sudden betrayals
and tighten him for slack moments.
"Life is a soft loam; be gentle; go easy."
And this too might serve him.
Brutes have been gentled where lashes failed.
The growth of a frail flower in a path up
has sometimes shattered and split a rock.
A tough will counts. So does desire.
So does a rich soft wanting.
Without rich wanting nothing arrives.
Tell him too much money has killed men
and left them dead years before burial:
the quest of lucre beyond a few easy needs
has twisted good enough men
sometimes into dry thwarted worms.
Tell him time as a stuff can be wasted.
Tell him to be a fool every so often
and to have no shame over having been a fool
yet learning something out of every folly
hoping to repeat none of the cheap follies

7 *Carl Sandburg lived from 1878-1967. Some of his works have received Pulitzer Prizes, and Sandburg had a middle school named after him. In this poem, a father is thinking about the advice he wishes to impart to his son.*

Tell him to be alone often and get at himself
and above all tell himself no lies about himself
whatever the white lies and protective fronts
he may use against other people.
Tell him solitude is creative if he is strong
and the final decisions are made in silent rooms.
Tell him to be different from other people
if it comes natural and easy being different.
Let him have lazy days seeking his deeper motives.
Let him seek deep for where he is born natural.
Then he may understand Shakespeare
and the Wright brothers, Pasteur, Pavlov,
Michael Faraday and free imaginations
Bringing changes into a world resenting change.
He will be lonely enough
to have time for the work
he knows as his own.

A Cradle Song

By William Blake

Sweet dreams form a shade
O'er my lovely infant's head;
Sweet dreams of pleasant streams
By happy, silent, moony beams.

Sweet sleep with soft down
Sleep sleep, happy child,
All creation slept and smil'd;
Sleep sleep, happy sleep,
While o'er thee thy mother weep.

Sweet babe, in thy face
Holy image I can trace.
Sweet babe, once like thee,
Thy maker lay and wept for me,

Wept for me for thee for all,
When he was an infant small.
Thou his image ever see.
Heavenly face that smiles on thee,

Smiles on thee on me on all,
Who became an infant small,
Infant smiles are His own smiles,
Heaven & earth to peace beguiles.

INDEX

Amanda Bradley........................20
Angela Morgan 97
antidote...13
Author Unknown13, 16, 18, 20, 59, 70, 71, 74
battles 14
Beaten..14
bird..16, 96
book...................................ii, iii, 22, 108
brother...........................28, 45, 46, 47
business 13
candle..16
Carl Sandburg...............................100
child.............................17, 51, 60, 102
children ....vi, 27, 33, 60, 63, 68, 95
courage30, 36, 37, 46, 49, 53, 67, 71, 72, 73, 85
cry......................................24, 56, 77
Dale Wimbrow 54
dare 14, 15, 24, 61, 93
daughter 28, 32
day10, 25, 26, 28, 32, 34, 35, 36, 39, 45, 50, 51, 54, 63, 66, 73, 76, 77, 78, 94
Death...26
decisions.....................30, 32, 84, 101
depression 45
Diane Loomans 17
divine 15, 97
Douglas Malloch........................43
dream7, 16, 20, 42, 53, 54, 61, 66, 68, 93
Dream...............................20, 53
earn 41
Earth 9

Edgar................11, 24, 36, 37, 39, 57
Ella Wheeler Wilcox 75, 78, 87
Emily Dickinson.............................96
face.........vi, 11, 34, 55, 58, 77, 87, 103
faith.........24, 37, 45, 53, 54, 76, 78, 81
Fion Lim....................................72, 84
flower 16, 50, 51, 52, 79, 101
fools..8, 101
forgive 41, 42
Frank Outlaw 57
Fred Burks 64
friendships 31, 33
future 19, 22, 23, 56, 76
game..23, 24
George Eliot................................34
give7, 13, 14, 19, 22, 23, 42, 44, 61, 73, 80, 88, 99
goal..................................16, 20, 24
Godvi, 15, 53, 54, 58, 60, 61, 67, 68, 78, 81
grandparents....................................33
happiness19, 27, 44, 49, 66, 75, 76, 86
health 19
heart8, 17, 26, 34, 41, 48, 51, 53, 54, 61, 73, 79, 85, 93
Helen Steiner Rice.....................53
help..........22, 31, 42, 67, 77, 80, 88, 89
hope....................16, 38, 44, 66, 78, 96
hugs...32, 73
hurt.........................8, 26, 49, 67, 73
ill 15, 37
impostors..8
inspiration..................................26, 83
investigate 41
Jessie B. Rittenhouse 56

Jim Rohn 55
Joaquin Miller...........15
John McLeod 28
Joseph Norris 40
journey...........16, 29, 30, 77, 87
Kent M. Keith...............88
kind 26, 34, 42, 80
Langston Hughes 99
laugh 16, 23, 74
lies 7, 70, 84, 90, 101
life8, 17, 21, 30, 31, 32, 39, 49, 50, 51,
  52, 53, 54, 55, 56, 57, 58, 62, 63, 66,
  73, 76, 77, 78, 81, 84, 86, 88, 93, 98,
  99, 100
Life14, 23, 25, 29, 30, 33, 35, 57, 83,
  99, 101
listen.................31, 41, 42
lla Wheeler Wilcox 77
Lord.....................14
loss........................8
loyalty 49
Lucille Clifton 98
Marianne Williamson 60
marriage 33
Maya Angelou..................90
mind.................19, 22, 38, 55, 80
mistakes...............19, 84
morning.............10, 32, 40, 97
mother 28, 32, 46, 99, 103
Nan Terrell Reed 35
Oriah Mountain Dreamer.61, 92
parents......................33
past..............19, 22, 25, 27
poor 13, 36, 37
Promise 19
prosperity..................19
rich 13, 37, 73, 101
Robert Frost 10

Rudyard Kipling 7
save......................42
sing..............11, 12, 78
smilevi, 13, 14, 16, 18, 19, 22, 39, 40,
  45, 50, 91
son 9, 28, 46, 99, 100, 101
song..............16, 49, 77, 78
star...............16, 40, 43
Steve Maraboli 26
stolen...................13
stronger 14
Success..............18, 48
sunbeam 16
Tanja Cilia 81
think8, 14, 19, 23, 31, 38, 39, 41, 53,
  69, 74, 90
thoughts................8, 57
tomorrow............32, 66, 74, 89
touch 8, 16, 73, 91
traveling..................29
tree 16, 18, 43, 50, 51
truth 8, 58, 68, 79
try 36, 41, 53, 59, 75, 91
Unknown23, 30, 32, 44, 45, 46, 48,
  50
virtue..............8, 79, 80
vote.....................16
Walter D. Wintle 14
water 40, 82
whine................23, 38
William Arthur Ward........41, 42
William Blake 102
William Ernest Henley.............86
wisdom 17, 29, 53, 65, 67
word 8, 16, 34
world22, 24, 36, 37, 50, 51, 54, 55, 58,
  60, 73, 81, 87, 90, 101
yesterday 27, 45, 66

Inspirational Poems

Cover and book design by AGORA BOOKS

Ultimate Inspirational Collection
volume 2
Motivational Poems
Keep yourself motivated
Inspiring and positive thinking

Check also our volume 1:

Inspirational Quotes:
Inspire, encourage and motivate yourself and others
http://amzn.com/1499579179

Printed in the United States of America
First Printing: May 2014

ISBN: 1499658435
ISBN-13: 978-1499658439